MY LIFE WITH HYDROCEPHALUS

MATTHEW E. PETCHINSKY

My Life with Hydrocephalus
Copyright © 2022 by Matthew E. Petchinsky

All rights reserved. No part of this publication
may be reproduced, distributed, or transmitted
in any form or by any means, including
photocopying, recording, or other electronic
or mechanical methods, without the prior
written permission of the author, except
in the case of brief quotations embodied
in critical reviews and certain other non-
commercial uses permitted by copyright law.

Tellwell Talent
www.tellwell.ca

ISBN
978-0-2288-8533-7 (Hardcover)
978-0-2288-8532-0 (Paperback)
978-0-2288-8534-4 (eBook)

Introduction

A bit of history about Hydrocephalus, Hydrocephalus is a name that the Greek gave the condition, it has been known on record as early as the fifth century by the ancients with Hippocrates. However, there isn't to say that other ancient civilizations knew of hydrocephalus. It is possible they did but did not record it due to them killing the young baby with hydrocephalus because of the large cranium. Malformations such as this were cause for fear back then and millions of children were killed for it. Like a mother animal killing her own weak and sicken young.

What is Hydrocephalus? You may be asking; well Hydrocephalus is a condition where there is an obstruction in the skull where the spot where cerebral spinal fluid is drained at the base of the skull is smaller than normal. This obstruction of the skull causes the normal cerebral spinal fluid to over fill in the places of the brain called ventricles. The ventricles are normally there in everyone, but others have it when they over fill with fluid which causes them to grow and cause the skull to become enlarged.

The rate in which children are born with hydrocephalus is some where around two of every thousand births in the United States alone, the only current treatment of Hydrocephalus is a VP shunt or ventriculoperitoneal shunt- a shunt that move fluid from the ventricles of the brain to the abdominal cavity.

- A ventriculoatrial shunt- this shunt moves fluid from the ventricles of the brain to a chamber of the heart.
- A lumboperitoneal shunt- this shunt moves fluid from the lower back to the abdominal cavity.

Even though these shunts are available for use and treatment, most places around the world much like India or other poorer countries don't place the shunt in the child right away until it is too late, and their head is already grown to a great size. Most die from hydrocephalus if not treated in time.

The average cost of the typical shunt surgery is somewhere between $35,816 to about $85,000 or more depending on the insurance company you are on to include the location you are having the surgery in United States.

There is a group out there called the Hydrocephalus Association, I have provided their website below:

Hydrocephalus Association | We're Here To Support You (hydroassoc.org)

This group meets in Austin, Texas every year for the Hydro walk, where they raise money for Hydrocephalus and a convention each year as well. There are only two awareness months of Hydrocephalus:

September is National Hydrocephalus month. The color is blue.

October is also known as the Texas Hydrocephalus month.

I am going to give for my lifetime experience with Hydrocephalus, my goal is to open people's mind and help bring better awareness about Hydrocephalus.

My Story

I know there have been many times in my life that I have felt weak because of the shunt in my head. Living every day with a such a device can be pain staking. Always avoiding strenuous activities such as lifting heavy objects, karate, boxing, basketball, football, Etc.

Being careful not to bump on hard objects, a life of caution is what I have lived to the best of my ability. I have been viewed differently all my life, I have a learning disability from the hydrocephalus and have developed many fears and phobias from having a shunt in my head. One big fear I've had was that I would be hit in the head with a stray basketball or get hit in the head with another student's backpack like I have seen other students do to each other.

I have protected myself from many things, that many of you find "fun and enjoyable" for example like rock climbing could lead to where I slip and fall and damage the shunting or another example scuba diving could be bad due to the cranium pressures could cause damage to the shunting.

I have developed a fear of riding a bicycle, because I don't want to damage the shunting. I have developed to a sensitivity to heat and the cold. For example, in the summer the weather is 102 degrees outside, my head begins to get a sharp pain and feel like my head is boiling to where the shunting starts to hurt as well. When it comes to winter and the temperature is 36 degrees or lower, even in the 40-degree weather, shunting starts to hurt as well to where is feels like I've been hit in the head.

Because all of this, I have viewed as "not normal". I have been bullied for being different and all the people I've explained the shunt to looked at me differently and believed that I am ridiculous for protecting the shunting.

I have been treated differently my entire life to where everyone from my stepparents to school officials have viewed me as "retarded" or "special Needs". Yes, Hydrocephalus does cause damage to the brain, especially areas of the brain to where it is hard to comprehend certain things that you need to explain it a few more times, but doesn't everyone have a learning disability? Math is hard to understand, and yes you must explain somethings twice, but that doesn't make a person with hydrocephalus "retarded" and dumb or weak. I have been viewed as a weak person and not human, place in a class of other special needs kids that have nothing truly in common with me. I was not like them.

During the times, I was in school and when I was living with my parents as well, I was treated as if I was nothing, not a human, not with a heart and mind or even a soul. I read books that were far beyond what they wanted me to read that kept me in a low reading level. I've even written early versions of stories that I had to destroy because my parents discouraged me from becoming an author.

Speaking of my so-called family, here is a bit of background, my biological father was in the military and my biological mother was a cheater and worker at retail stores. They both divorced when I was six years old. My Dad's friend who later became my stepdad was a jerk and bully and as well as my biological mother. Remember how I told you I tried to protect the back of my head where the shunt was? Well, my stepdad and biological mom hit me several times back there, hard enough to cause pain in the shunting itself. No one believed me of course, why would you believe a child that is deemed not human, right?

My biological father was a tough man, he believed grades were everything and he would beat me for 70's and lower when I have a learning disability.

Now, this wasn't a belt type of beating or hand. Oh no that's too "soft" for him. He took me out in the garage and had me bend over a chair and beat my butt with a block of 2x4 wood about a foot or foot and a half long. To this day, I am suffering the consequences of his rage, I found out that I have a pinched nerve between my S1 and L5 vertebra on my spine.

Which is quite funny no other doctor picked this up in their scan, but the ones here in Eagle Pass have from a CT scan.

My Stepmother was very condescending and rude to me, making me her house maid to clean her home because that is all she thought I was good for. She thought I was faking when it came to shunt pains as well as my biological dad and everyone else in my so-called family.

I must apologize to you dear reader, a lot of this will me be me unloading my trauma that I have built up in my lifetime with the hydrocephalus. Trauma and anger are another thing that has occurred in my lifetime with the hydrocephalus.

My Stepmom called me "retarded" and "autistic" on several occasions because I could not process what she was saying, her English didn't make sense at times because she is Turkish, I've even been called "retard" in Turkish too. My Entire life has been full of bullying in school and at home.

I don't know if others are going through the same things as me. I just have this to say, no matter how much you feel compelled to bully someone that is different than you, don't because one day they may be the ones to help you.

When it came to doctors, there was one in Austin, Texas, I would go see. Dr. Patricia Aronin. I have known her since I was six years old. She kept telling me for years how the shunting looking fine and intact. I mentioned many, many times that I wanted that old shunt out and that it didn't feel right. Of course, she like others didn't believe me. Also, as well as quite a few factors such as me going between parents got in the way of my health. Dr. Aronin wanted to do a shunt injection. A shunt injection is a procedure when a liquid die is injected in the valve of the shunting to clarify if it is functional, by MRI or X Ray scan where the die is visible. I've done regular MRI scans, but they never showed anything wrong with the shunting.

A few things that I feel while having the shunting in my head is the pain around the shunting not only when it is hot or cold outside, but when I was trying to think on how to solve math problems in school, I felt tugging of the tubing down my neck and into my abdomen. The tugging was more like someone on the other end trying to rip it out, there was sharp rubbing in the neck and abdomen area. Headaches were quite often to where I couldn't focus on school and had to get home (and yes, I got in trouble for having to go home early for that too, even though I wasn't faking and truly not feeling well). These headaches went away after some 800mg of Motrin also known as Ibuprofen (military grade, had to take 2 of them).

These headaches happened every day, how could I fake a headache that felt like someone just split my head open with a saw? Of course, my parents had it and stopped coming to pick me up at school, but the headaches never did stop. I had to learn to tolerate the pain of the headaches that almost lead me to pass out and vomit as well.

Sleeping at night with the shunting, even now is difficult. The shunt makes itself well known even with the most comfortable pillow. It feels as though my right side of my head is lifted an inch off the pillow, making a very uncomfortable experience.

With the Hydrocephalus already leaving me with a weaken immune system. I was and am even more susceptible to diseases and illnesses. I've had pneumonia over a dozen or so times each year when I was a kid, Bronchitis every year for about the same amount of time. I've had several kidney stones as well. I believe that hydrocephalus does cause the immune system to be weak because it is attacking the brain when helps regulate the immune system as well.

Oh, I have developed diabetes insipidus to where my kidney isn't getting the signal to stop taking in water. I feel constant thirst as well and have a urinary issue. My doctor believes it must do with the shunt surgeries.

I know hydrocephalus can cause seizures as well, I believe I have had seizures without knowing it as a kid, now as an adult, I developed full blown seizures as well, especially when I get over stressed or a nightmare. I do have where there are times where I get really irritable, along with extreme fatigue, as well as the inability to eat as well. Depression and anxiety are common with me and I'm sure with other with hydrocephalus as well. Speaking of other health issues, there has been a kidney infection as well. My entire life has been full of health issues, abuse, and being treated like a thing, a nonhuman.

My Hydrocephalus journey is still going to this day. Everyday is a struggle with the shunting and highly stressing because you never know if the shunting is going to malfunction and fail on you.

Years went by same thing repeatedly; my trauma and abuse grew more and more. The stress levels were taking their toll on the shunting. While on a cruise in Alaska, the shunt tubing snapped in my neck. There was nothing that could be done when that happened. We were hundreds of miles away from the nearest major hospital, but that wasn't the main problem. My parents didn't believe me that I felt a sharp pain in my neck prior to the shunt tubing snapping. I do recall feeling the initial snapping of the tubing as well. They pushed it to the side as unimportant as every health issue with me, because they thought I was ruining their fun, as well as the next week I had an appointment with Dr. Aronin, but what if I had died on the cruise?

Well for one I wouldn't be here to write this story. The next week came, and we were back in San Antonio, Texas on our way to Austin. When we got there, Dr. Aronin had me lay down on an examination table in an MRI or X Ray room, I remember hold someone's hand because of my nervousness.

Dr. Aronin injected the die in my shunting and found that she couldn't get fluid to go either direction because the shunt has calcified.

This is interesting part; calcification is where the calcium salts that normally form bone builds up in the tissues of the body. The way I figure it is that my body thought the shunting was soft tissue, so it deposited the calcium along the shunting, after years of this build up cause the shunting to be unless. My body was giving me signs for years, the tugging and pains were signs, but Dr. Aronin kept saying everything looked "fine".

During the shunt injection, the scan did prove that the tubing did snap. I believe that the shunt tubing couldn't handle the weight of calcium build up and it broke.

The next test that was done on me since the shunt was nonfunctioning, was where the opened a part of my skull and place a pressure monitor in my head. I have a deep incision point in the front of my skull above my right side of my forehead, where they had pressure monitoring device was place. The device itself was a monitor with a long wire that is to be placed inside the skull. The scale on which the used is if the numbers read in the negatives on the monitor, it is good, but if they go into the positives by raising pressures on the inside the skull indicates a problem. Pressures in the skull can change due to getting angry to straining to use the restroom as what was noticed on pressure monitoring screen. The wiring of the device does move inside the skull on occasion that you feel like something crawling inside your skull. The movement isn't a normal function of the device it is because nothing on the inside of the skull is keeping them in place.

After a few days of the pressure monitoring device in my head. I had a surgery to remove the old shunting from my head. When I got back to the patient room, there was a specimen cup with a piece of the old shunt tubing in it. The tubing was leaking black fluid and has signs of damage and was very disturbing to see.

When I saw the tubing, I felt a relief with the shunting out of my head and was hoping to have peace from it as well. When I asked Dr. Aronin why she saved a sample of the shunt tubing. She said that she thought I would want to see it. Honestly, I did not want to see it, I just wanted to never feel the shunting in my head again. I would have preferred that all those pieces of the old shunt to be destroyed. I threw that piece of the old shunt tubing away of course. If I were to keep it, wouldn't that seem a bit strange to keep? I didn't want to have a constant remind that I didn't already have, such as the scars that I have on my body. Why would I need an extra reminder?

I have several scars on my body from the shunt surgery, even the original one that was from 1993. The scars are a constant remind of the shunt surgery, dealing and living with these scars are a daily thing in living with Hydrocephalus. Sometimes the scars lead to body image issues to where you don't want to go to the pool in swim trunks without a shirt. Or fear that your boyfriend or girlfriend will get disgusted with your body and reject you because of the scars. These are true thoughts that I've had before when I was dating, I've since then got comfortable with my body for the most part.

Now, these was a time where I went two years without the shunting, the first thing that happened was when we went to an MRI scan in 2012 the same year of the shunt removal, the scan showed my ventricles growing a bit. This scared Dr. Aronin to where she suggested we put a new pressure monitor device in. she just wanted to make sure things went well. There was a chance that I could have had a new shunt in my head again in December of 2012.

During that time with the new pressure monitor everything seemed to go well, so we dodged the bullet so to speak for the moment on getting a new shunt. Also, on another note the same spot when the first pressure monitor was reopened and placed a new one in it. When it came to getting to be discharge, you would think you would go to an operation room to get it removed, right?

Wrong, Dr. Aronin, personally herself pulled the pressure monitor wiring out of my head in the patient room in very un-sanitized conditions (being that I have been in the room for five days straight). She then just placed a bandaged on the spot with out closing off the incision site that the pressure monitor wiring was in. I did feel pain as the wiring was being pulled out of my head. Dr. Aronin of course disregarded it as not true. She said, "You won't feel pain as it is being removed". Right, in some opposite world with no pain senses in it. The skull is full of nerve ending that sense pain in it. Why is it that neurologists and many other doctors believe the brain doesn't feel pain?

The recovery from the shunt surgeries is when you need to keep the areas where the scars will form clean 2 times a day, bath from the hips down, don't get incision sites wet for a period of two months. No lifting heavy objects as well or any activity that could lead to incision sites to reopen. Sometimes you need help cleaning the sites from the surgery, but if you are clever enough to find away to clean the sites from the surgery. I used the bathroom mirror and my iPod touch at the time to clean and bandage my incision site on the back of my head.

There is a scar on my belly just below the original scar that was reopened twice, it was sealed both time with super glue. I am surprised that super glue is used for cuts, but isn't super glue not good for the skin?

I have had nightmares three separate times about having shunt surgery. One time before the removal of the shunt, one three months after the shunt was removed and the third was five or six months before the shunt was put back in my head. All three nightmares were the same result of me dying in the dream. I know the whole shunt surgery process causes anxiety and stress which lead to the nightmares being produced.

I went two years without the shunt in my head, but there were signs where I needed a new shunt, such as:

- memory loss
- loss of balance
- oversleeping at certain points in the day
- having trouble concentrating while doing schoolwork for college.
- extreme headaches

Each of these happened to me, let me explain how each one happened.

The memory loss was where I forget things that I remembered for years and as well things I was just told three seconds before. That was worse than regular short term memory loss, that usually is a few minutes slower not three seconds.

Loss of balance was where I couldn't walk straight or focus, sort of like someone spinning you around and around several times then letting you go to walk all dizzy like. That is how I felt, during this whole process.

Oversleeping at certain points, well sometimes it can't be help some of the time, but mine was almost every day. I didn't stay up late or anything at night. I was for example sleeping on the VIA Bus (public transportation) when I missed my stop in the morning and afternoon when heading home from the college. I even missed my alarms for work as well.

I may have a learning disability which typically made learning difficult, but it seems when my head was hurting from the pressure that my head was going to explode when I tried to focus on schoolwork.

My headaches were extreme to the point that I got dizzy and felt like passing out from the pain. The headaches got worse each day.

I had an IQ test done and MRI. I don't understand what hydrocephalus and an IQ test have to do with each other, but for some reason Dr. Aronin ordered one. We did learn that the MRI scan showed that my ventricles in the brain were enlarged and causing these problems. If it had not been caught in time, I possibly could have died in my sleep or something.

I in fact was not happy to hear that I would have to go back to having a shunt in my head, after wanting it out for 18 years. I had a "short vacation" you could say.

Dr. Aronin told me that I would have to have the shunt back in my head and of course my rage boiled forward and I kept from releasing my rage, but Dr. Aronin must have seen the look on my face, knowing that I was upset. She said in front of my dad that I could hit her to let out my rage. I of course did not, who says that? I know that if I had done so she would have had me arrested for assault. I told her that I would not do that, it was my body working against me, possible all the stress I subjected to between my job, school, the constant nagging by my stepmom and dad for my spending or whatever they saw fit to nag about. Yes, my stepmom who worked at the bank was spying on my bank account everyday and nagging on my spending habits. Sorry, got a bit off topic there. The point is that it was not Dr. Aronin's fault that the ventricles were filling up. My battle with hydrocephalus was not over like I thought it was. It is like an enemy striking at peaceful times without announcing itself to take it's target off guard. Which is exactly how hydrocephalus was acting.

A few moments after the appointment, we stopped at a store, and I was alone in the car furious that I was going to have to have the shunt back in my head again. I recalled bursting into tears from how upset I was. I felt betrayed by my body, I didn't want the shunt back in my body, I slept better without the shunt in my head for two years, I didn't feel a pressure on the back of my head from where the shunting was placed those two years without it.

I had to get a two-week time period to get things situated with my job to get time off for this major surgery, although there was a chance I might not come out of this alive.

The procedure is very risky, it is open head surgery essentially to place the shunt inside.

From what I remember, I was working at a store named Thrift Town. I had been working with them at the time since September of 2013 and I was there only there a few months before the surgery was to happen. I had gathered a considerable amount of paid time off that I was planning to use for the surgery, it was rejected several times, but I still needed the time off and they raddled off something that I am not eligible for FMLA, But I was not asking for FMLA, I was asking for a week of my PTO to be used. They even threatened to fire me, but I stood firm and of course, told them that this surgery is important, and it only requires a week off, I am not sure what happened after, but I did get the PTO approved. The stress from that gave me a large headache and cause an anxiety attack as well, because I had never been threatened to be fired before. Looking back at it now, I see my anxiety was misplaced because I was younger and didn't really realize that the job wasn't the only one I could have, but it was difficult for me to get other jobs at the time, I should have let them fire me, the $7.45 an hour wasn't worth wasting my breath to save my crap job for after this major surgery.

When everything was situated in place for the week of the surgery, I had a bag pack for the week with DVDs and other things like phone charger and book as well as clothes for when I will be out of hospital. I spend a week with the new shunt in my head, they wanted to see if anything was going to go wrong like my body rejecting the shunting, which is the common for the most part where in most cases from what I've read that the person had to go back into surgery because of the shunt rejection. I fortunately didn't have that problem. I had the movie Independence Day (1996) playing for 24 hours, it was the special edition with extra few minutes of film as well. The nurses noticed and were shocked on why it was in there for so long. I couldn't move from the bed to change it, being that I had an IV in my arm and the pressure monitor in my head as well again in the same spot as the first two times.

I do recall that Dr. Aronin saying that she left the old catheter from the old shunt in my head from the last time because of the calcification made it suck, so she had to drill into it to put a new catheter in. She also said this last shunt surgery was three and a half hours long, and they had to do multiply scans while I was under anesthesia, she said there was a lot of scar tissue as well, they even reopened the scar that is under the original scar that was made two years prior with the shunt removal. I have been over the medical records several times, why does it not mention any of that or are the records I have a copy of not complete, because my parents did say they had trouble locating them all.

After that week of being in the hospital, it was the same thing again of two months of no normal showering or strenuous activity. I do recall after the first day of me returning to work I had to go home within the first few hours because of a massive headache that almost made me pass out, being that I have gotten used to these headaches as a child being in school, I was trying to actually push through to stay at work, but it got bad and I couldn't handle it anymore, that I had to go home.

It took about two or three weeks to readjust back to having the shunt in my head (honestly for the last 8 years, the shunt still bothers me). I can tell you about the date for each shunt surgery I've had, there are three of them:

- October 20th, 1993, my birthday (first shunt)
- July 5th, 2012, shunt removal.
- July 15th, 2014, new shunt was put in.

I have the last two dates marked on my calendar on my phone and I have it set to remind me each time. It is quite strange that from the time of removal to the new shunt is exactly two years and ten days apart. I have always found that time period to be a bit of a coincidence. Why would that long of a time span, isn't that just strange?

One main point I would like to make, when it comes to those that have hydrocephalus, they need support of friends and family because this is a tough process, like how most of the time I was alone throughout this process especially with my parents not having to be there all the time and my step grandma was there a little bit of the time but even she couldn't be there entirely because of her own health issues. My biological mother and stepdad were never there, they went to Hawaii during that time and came up with a bull of an answer that "they couldn't move the trip dates". She came to visit two weeks after the procedure, but that was a side stop with her heading to visit her mother in south Texas. My stepmom's brother and his family were there, I barely knew them. I know life is hard and things can't be changed but to know that you care for someone that has hydrocephalus and especially with a major surgery is important to have support. Emotions run high with this procedure. What if that surgery failed and this was the last time you got to see someone you know that has hydrocephalus, would you really go to Hawaii then?

Also, when you have a new boyfriend or girlfriend or friend for that matter it is hard to explain what hydrocephalus is and you do fear they will see you less than you are. Many people I've said that I have hydrocephalus and a shunt in my head, act differently around me because they don't know if I am the same person that they met a week ago before I told them this health issue. Yes, I am still that same person, nothing has changed, other than you know my health issue.

I even had an Ex-girlfriend tell her mom and she told her that since I have hydrocephalus, I would be a bad boyfriend and couldn't balance school, a job and relationship.

Now, that is incorrect information that she was given of course. Hydrocephalus maybe difficult on the person who has it and the family or whoever they may encounter because it is a worrisome thought of when the shunt fails, but for the most part people can live normal lives and have families, jobs, careers, or anything that they want if they remember to be careful and not do anything insane like cliff jumping or jumping out of a plane. Well, in general I wouldn't suggest those crazy things even for a person without a shunt as well.

There is a stigma attached to having hydrocephalus such as the one I mentioned above. My best advice for anyone who has hydrocephalus is to look beyond the stigma, believe in yourself and don't let anyone get you down. I believe hydrocephalus isn't getting as much attention nationally or internationally for that matter. There was a person that had videos a while ago on YouTube under the name Blue for Britney. She had since then removed her videos. Hydrocephalus needs it's place as big as cancer in the medical journals, from what I've read that there are approximately one million or more people in the United States alone, then with that many people with hydrocephalus, why isn't it mentioned much?

I am finding it difficult to find a proper neurologist that is knowledgeable enough about Hydrocephalus. The last one I had was confused and seemed not to understand anything about shunting as well. There needs to have a complete change in the medical schooling as well. Hydrocephalus is never going to go away, there are enough people that have it on this planet that it should be a well-known fact.

For those of you that have hydrocephalus, know that you are not alone and there is an entire community of people just like you. As well don't put yourself down, you can achieve great thing, look forward into the future and maintain your stress levels and take care of yourself. You are just as important as any other person, you are not a nonhuman, retard, or any of the mean things that are said to those of us with hydrocephalus.

My life with /hydrocephalus is a struggle, in fact the other night, I got a painful headache that cause shunt pains as well. I have tried to put an ice pack on the back of my head. If you do plan to put an ice pack on the back of your head where the shunt is, you could make things a little worse. I did that and felt a sharp shooting pain in my head where the shunt is.

Everyday is a struggle with Hydrocephalus, you never know when you are going to have a shunt pain or shunt headache. There is the tugging of the shunt tubing at certain points, or the worry that your shunt will fail from the everyday stresses. Seizures are common for those with Hydrocephalus, you can develop seizures at any point during your life with Hydrocephalus.

There is a book I recommend for anyone who has Hydrocephalus. The book also helps those that are living with a person that has Hydrocephalus. The book is called

Hydrocephalus: A guide for patients, families and friends.

The book I mentioned above has very great information for anyone who wants to understand what it is like with hydrocephalus.

Final words from the Author

Hello Everyone,

    I hope this book finds you well and it helps you understand better about Hydrocephalus, even if you have it or not. If you are a parent of someone who has Hydrocephalus, please make sure you keep up on the shunt checkups. I have seen photos where children have large heads because the parents and doctors don't understand Hydrocephalus. Please don't let your child have an enlarged skull because of Hydrocephalus. It is fatal without a shunt.

                                -Matthew Edward Petchinsky

Check out my first book, *Life of government benefits: my family's experience.*

You can find the book on Amazon and Barnes and Noble.

I appreciate you purchasing these books, thank you.

-Matthew Edward Petchinsky

www.ingramcontent.com/pod-product-compliance
Lightning Source LLC
LaVergne TN
LVHW041553060526
838200LV00037B/1265